J.K. ROWLING
CREATOR OF HARRY POTTER

Cath Senker

WAYLAND

Published in 2012 by Wayland

Copyright © Wayland 2012

Wayland
338 Euston Road
London NW1 3BH

Wayland Australia
Level 17/207 Kent Street
Sydney, NSW 2000

Senior editor: Camilla Lloyd
Designer: Rob Walster
Picture researcher: Shelley Noronha

Picture acknowledgments: The author
and publisher would like to thank the
following for allowing their pictures to
be reproduced in this publication: Cover
and 4: © WWD/Condé Nast/Corbis; ©
Chris Howes/WildPlaces Photography/
Alamy: 8; © Pictorial Press Ltd/Alamy: 15,
23, 24; © Stewart Mark, Camera Press:
5; © Ric Ergenbright/Corbis: 6; © Corbis
Sygma: 10; © Owen Franken/Corbis: 12;
© Matthias Tunger/Corbis: 17; © Reuters/
Corbis: 21, 25; © Rune Hellestad/Corbis:
27; © Jamie Fine/Reuters/Corbis: 29;
© Getty Images: 16, 22; ISTOCK: 14; ©
Nils Jorgensen/Rex Features: 9; © Stuart
Atkins/ Rex Features: 11; © Gavin Rogers/
Rex Features:18; © Marius Alexander/
Rex Features: 19; © Denis Jones/Evening
Standard/ Rex Features: 26; © Nick
Cunard/Rex Features: 28; © Topfoto: 7, 13;
© National News/Topfoto: 20.

British Library Cataloguing in
Publication Data:
Senker, Cath.
J.K. Rowling. – (Inspirational lives)
1. Rowling, J. K.–Juvenile literature. 2.
Women novelists, English–20th century–
Biography–Juvenile literature. 3. Novelists,
English–20th century–Biography–Juvenile
literature.
I. Title II. Series
823.9'14-dc22

ISBN: 978 0 7502 6954 4

Printed in China

Wayland is a division of Hachette
Children's Books, an Hachette UK
company.

www.hachette.co.uk

Contents

A flash of inspiration

Joanne Rowling, the creator of Harry Potter, has been writing stories since she was six years old. She has a wonderful imagination, and in her mind she travels back to her youth to invent her tales from a child's viewpoint.

J.K. Rowling's moment of inspiration occurred on a train journey when she was 25. After a weekend's flat hunting in Manchester, she was going back to London. Suddenly, the train broke down because of a fault, and the travellers were stuck for several hours. She says that while she was gazing out of the window at some cows, "the idea for Harry Potter simply fell into my head."

Jo was more excited about this idea than any she had ever had before.

WRITING TIPS

Always keep a notebook and pen with you for jotting down ideas for stories. Jo loves to collect unusual names for characters and places.

This is a portrait of J.K. Rowling in London in 2009, wearing a glamorous evening dress.

INSPIRATION

In a flash of inspiration, Jo saw an image of Harry Potter in her mind's eye – a skinny boy with tousled dark hair, round glasses and an extraordinary lightning-shaped scar on his forehead.

Journey beyond your imagination.

Harry Potter and the Philosopher's Stone

In this poster for the first Harry Potter film, you can see the young Harry (right) and some of his classmates and teachers. The towers of Hogwarts school loom in the background.

Jo didn't have a pen with her and was too shy to ask to borrow one. So for the entire four hours that the train was delayed, she sat quietly and dreamt up her ideas. Harry Potter came to life in her head – an orphan who finds out at the age of eleven that he is a talented wizard. He is invited to attend Hogwarts school for witches and wizards, in a wild and remote castle. Jo began to invent the rules of a complete magical world.

As soon as she arrived home, Jo started writing down her story. She was bursting with ideas for Harry's school life at Hogwarts. This story would run and run.

An imaginative child

J.K. Rowling had a fairly ordinary early childhood. Her parents, Peter and Anne, met while they were still teenagers and married at 19. They set up home in Yate, a small town near Bristol, England. Peter took a job in an aircraft factory while Anne prepared for the birth of their first child. Their daughter Joanne was born in 1965, and Dianne, usually known as Di, came along two years later.

This is Winterbourne Village in Dorset, where Jo lived as a child.

As a young child, Jo enjoyed playing imaginary games with her little sister. When Jo was four, the family moved to a house in Winterbourne, in Dorset, where the girls had plenty of space to play and act out adventures. Jo started writing stories when she was six. Her first one was called 'Rabbit and Miss Bee'. Jo says, "Ever since Rabbit and Miss Bee, I knew I wanted to be a writer."

INSPIRATION

Jo was fascinated by the classic children's book *The Wind in the Willows* by Kenneth Grahame. Her father read it to her when she had measles around the age of four and she remembers it vividly.

Peter and Anne were keen readers, and their house was full of books. They loved to read to Jo, and she delighted in all kinds of stories, including **fantasy** and **classic** tales. Her parents allowed their daughter to read whatever she liked.

When she wasn't reading or writing, Jo had fun playing outdoors with other local children. Two of her best early childhood friends were called Ian and Vikki Potter. She always liked the name Potter …

WRITING TIPS

Jo says to read as widely as you can to learn how different authors write. It will also help you to increase your **vocabulary** and improve your writing style.

Town and countryside in Tutshill

In 1974, when Jo was nine, the family moved to Tutshill, near Chepstow in Gloucestershire. It was a bustling small town, surrounded by beautiful countryside. Around this time, Jo's much-loved grandmother Kathleen died. Jo later adopted her initial when she became J.K. Rowling.

Jo started at a new school in Tutshill, which was hard at first. It was a strict school. She did badly in a test and was put in the 'stupid row'. Yet she studied hard and her marks began to improve. When Jo looks back, she feels she was seen as the serious daughter, wearing thick glasses and always with her nose in a book. Di was the pretty, lively daughter. Jo was quite insecure so she tried to do as well as possible at school to seem confident.

Ian Fleming created an exciting world for his hero, James Bond.

HONOURS BOARD

Books Jo loved as a child:
The Narnia series, C. S. Lewis
Manxmouse, Paul Gallico
The Little White Horse, Elizabeth Goudge
Books by E. Nesbit and Noel Streatfeild
Ian Fleming's *James Bond* novels

At primary school, Jo loved reading and was obsessed with writing. As she has said: "Writing for me is a kind of **compulsion**, so I don't think anyone could have made me do it, or prevented me from doing it. "

She worked hard on her writing and shared some of her stories with friends. Yet in general she was shy about her talents and didn't mention her ambition to be an author to other people.

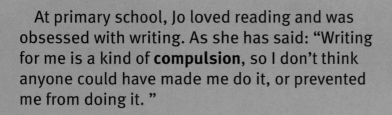

Jo arrives at the Albert Hall in London to sign copies of her book. Her hard work as a young writer eventually brought her fame.

Teenage years

When she was 11, Jo started at Wyedean Comprehensive School. She met new friends and made excellent progress in English and languages. During her teenage years, she grew less timid and more self-confident.

Jo read some of her tales to her new friends, who were very impressed. Teachers complimented her imaginative writing too. Yet a lot of her stories were never shared with anyone.

Jo continued to read widely. She was particularly keen on the early nineteenth-century author Jane Austen and was enthused by Jessica Mitford's **autobiography** *Hons and Rebels.*

A scene from a film of Jane Austen's novel, Sense and Sensibility. *Austen's novels feature young women with strong personalities.*

School life was going well, but when Jo was in her early teens, her home life took a turn for the worse. Her mother developed multiple sclerosis, a disease that attacks the nervous system. Anne's condition steadily worsened, and she grew increasingly disabled. It was a difficult time for the whole family. Jo's friends kept her spirits up, and she focused on reading, writing and studying.

Harry Potter and his friends in a magic Ford Anglia that can fly!

WRITING TIPS

Lucy Shepherd, Jo's favourite teacher at Wyedean said: "As a writer, you should **structure** your work and make sure you **pace** your story so it moves neither too quickly nor too slowly."

In her final year at school, Jo was so popular and successful in her studies that she was made head girl. At this time she became best friends with Sean Harris. He owned the original turquoise Ford Anglia that would later feature in the Harry Potter books. Sean was her first friend to learn to drive, and the pair went off for outings in his car. Jo confided in Sean her deepest wish to be a writer.

A secretary's story

After finishing school in 1983, Jo went to Exeter University, in south-west England. Her parents had advised her to study French although she would have preferred to take English. The plus side to the course was the year she spent in Paris perfecting her French. While at university, Jo spent much of her free time reading and improving her writing. After four years she successfully finished her degree. Then she needed to find a job.

Jo wasn't confident enough to try to have her stories published. Without a clear career plan, she moved to London and took a secretarial course for people with language skills. Then for two years she worked as a researcher for the human rights organisation Amnesty International. She did various secretarial jobs after leaving Amnesty.

The Sorbonne University in Paris, where Jo studied for a year as part of her French course.

INSPIRATION

The main characters in the Harry Potter books are Harry, Hermione and Ron. Harry and Hermione are both like Jo in some way. Harry is serious, while Hermione is intelligent and hardworking. Ron is partly inspired by Jo's friend Sean Harris – very loyal to his friends.

In 1990, Jo and her boyfriend decided to move to Manchester, and Jo took a secretarial job at the Manchester Chamber of Commerce. It was at this time that she started writing the story of Harry Potter. She filled all her spare moments creating his world.

Harry Potter lives part of his life in the regular, non-magical '**Muggle**' world, and the rest in the wizarding community, along with ghosts, goblins and magical creatures. He flies a broomstick, casts spells and makes potions. Harry becomes part of the continuous struggle of the wizarding world against the menace of evil wizards.

WOW!

Jo was a terrible secretary. She used to daydream in meetings and think up characters for her story.

When Harry Potter discovers he is a wizard, he is amazed to find he has a talent for flying on a broomstick!

Life in Portugal

In December 1990, just after Jo's family celebrated Christmas together, Anne Rowling died of multiple sclerosis, aged only 45. Even though she had been ill, it was still a terrible shock. Jo was stricken by grief and could no longer focus on her office work.

She decided it was time for a clean break. A few months after her mother's death, she set off to a new job teaching English in Oporto, Portugal. Jo enjoyed life in sunny Portugal, where she soon made friends. Her classes were in the afternoons and evenings so she had plenty of time in the mornings to write. She had great fun inventing all of Harry's adventures.

WRITING TIPS

Jo says you should plan your storyline before you start writing. But do leave some elements to be decided along the way. It's more fun like that.

The city of Oporto in Portugal, where Jo worked as an English teacher for about two years.

While working as a teacher, she met and fell in love with journalism student Jorge Arantes. In 1992 they were married, and shortly afterwards, Jo became pregnant. She was overjoyed when her daughter Jessica was born; however, the relationship between Jo and Jorge was failing. Unfortunately, a few months later, the couple split up. Jo had no idea what to do or where to go next.

The young wizard, Harry (centre) discovers more about his magical powers in Harry Potter and the Philosopher's Stone.

INSPIRATION

After the trauma of her mother's death, Jo gained a greater understanding of how Harry Potter would feel about his parents who died when he was a baby. Her own insights helped her to develop Harry's character. In Portugal she wrote the chapter 'The Mirror of Erised'. In the mirror, people see their deepest desire. Harry sees his parents waving at him.

A day in the life of J.K. Rowling

No two days are the same for Jo, but this imaginary schedule gives you an idea of the demands on her time in recent years.

J.K. Rowling reads from The Tales of Beedle the Bard.

7 am Wakes up and helps her children to get ready for school.

9 am Writes in her office at home.

Reads letters from charities asking for donations. Deals with correspondence from the charities she supports.

12.30 pm Lunch meeting with the people who run Gingerbread. Jo offers much support to this charity for one-parent families.

2 pm Goes to a primary school to give a book reading.

3.30 pm to 8 pm Spends time with her family.

8.30 pm Fundraising dinner for the charity Multiple Sclerosis Society in Scotland.

HONOURS BOARD

Time it took Jo to:

Write *Harry Potter and the Philosopher's Stone*: 5 years

Get her first novel published: 2 years

Write the entire Harry Potter series: 17 years

A boy chooses a book. Jo always dreamt of seeing her books on sale.

There are many stages in the writing process. Jo plans out the plot and develops the characters, working out complete histories for most of them. She thinks of unusual and interesting names for the people, creatures and objects in her stories.

Jo always writes in longhand first. She likes to shuffle papers around. Later, she copies her work on to a computer. After **drafting** each chapter, she **edits** it several times until she is satisfied with it. She sends the completed manuscript to the publishers. The editor checks the text and may ask her to make changes and correct any mistakes.

WRITING TIPS

Jo says there is no perfect recipe for a good story but some important ingredients are: humour, strong characters and a carefully thought-out plot.

Difficult times

In December 1993, Jo moved to Edinburgh, Scotland, where her sister Di lived. She hoped to find a job, but she could not afford childcare for Jessica. She decided to take a huge risk. She would remain out of work for a year, relying on **welfare benefits**, and finish her Harry Potter novel.

The owners of this café claim that Jo wrote Harry Potter here. Yet she spent much of her time writing in the Nicolson Café next door.

INSPIRATION

Di has always encouraged her sister's story-telling. Once Jo had completed three chapters of Harry Potter, she showed them to Di, who laughed out loud. If Di hadn't enjoyed reading the book, Jo might never have finished writing it.

Jo was short of money, living in a tiny flat with her baby. Writing Harry's tale kept her cheerful, as did support from Di and a few loyal friends. She developed a writing routine. She used to go for a walk with the baby in the pushchair. Once Jessica was asleep, she headed to the Nicolson Café, co-owned by Dougal McBride. He commented: "She was quite an odd sight. She would just push the pram and write away."

J.K. Rowling in 1999, writing in a café. She found it hard to write at home.

By late 1995, the novel was complete. Jo typed out the entire 90,000-word **manuscript** twice on a typewriter. She sent it to a **literary agent**, who rejected it. Then she sent it to another agent, Christopher Little. He loved it and was determined to find a publisher. Jo was not ambitious or driven by money – she simply wished to see her book on a shelf in a bookshop. She prepared herself for possible rejection.

WOW!

A mystery friend whose name has never been revealed helped Jo in 1995. She'd applied to take a teacher training course so she could teach modern languages in schools but couldn't afford childcare. This kind friend offered her a loan. Jo worried about whether she would make enough money to pay her friend back.

Harry Potter and the Philosopher's Stone

In August 1996, Jo's manuscript was finally accepted by Bloomsbury publishers. Jo was absolutely delighted but she continued her normal life. Having completed her teacher training, she started a teaching job.

WRITING TIPS

When you start writing, it's a good idea to begin with your own life. Write about your own experiences and feelings.

As the publication date drew near, Bloomsbury publishers asked if they could publish the book under the name J.K. Rowling. They were worried that young boys would be put off by a woman author. Jo didn't mind at all – as long as the book came out.

When *Harry Potter and the Philosopher's Stone* arrived in bookshops in June 1997, it proved an immediate hit with children. A **reviewer** in the Scottish newspaper, *The Glasgow Herald* was typical, saying, "I have yet to find a child who can put it down. Magic stuff." Adults were enchanted too.

A child wearing Harry Potter-style glasses enjoys the first Harry Potter novel.

Publishers abroad soon learnt of the stunning success of the Harry Potter title and were keen to publish it in their own countries. In the USA, Arthur A. Levine of Scholastic Press loved the book and was prepared to take a massive gamble. He offered $105,000 (£65,000) for the **rights** to publish it in the USA. This was an unheard-of sum in the children's publishing world at that time. Jo realised this deal would change her life. She decided to become a full-time writer.

Her 'rags to riches' tale soon became well-known, and many magazines and newspapers asked for interviews. It was quite scary for Jo being thrust into the limelight. Whenever possible, she asked reporters to interview her at a table in the homely Nicolson Café.

J.K. Rowling proudly shows off her OBE in 2001. She received this award for her writing.

HONOURS BOARD

Awards for *Harry Potter and the Philosopher's Stone* in 1998:

British Book Awards: Children's Book of the Year

Children's Book Award

Nestlé Smarties Gold Award 9–11 years

Catapulted to fame

Jo was now working on volume two, *Harry Potter and the Chamber of Secrets*. In the book, Harry's young wizard friends, the Weasleys, help him to escape his awful Muggle relatives in a Ford Anglia. An **anti-racist** theme runs through the story. When pure-blooded wizards attack those from mixed wizarding and Muggle backgrounds, Harry and his friends try to stop them.

Jo stuck to her normal routine, writing in cafés. However, in 1997 she did move to a larger, more comfortable home. She no longer needed to worry about having enough money to bring up her daughter.

In July 1998, *Harry Potter and the Chamber of Secrets* was published.

It went straight to the top of the **bestseller** lists. Now, Bloomsbury drew up a **contract** for Jo to write a total of seven Harry Potter titles. Sensibly, she planned out the remaining five to ensure she could write them all. For her it was a pleasure: "I love writing these books. I don't think anyone

J.K. Rowling signs a copy of her book for a fan in New York, USA, in October 2009.

could enjoy reading them more than I enjoy writing them."

The following month, the first Harry Potter book came out in the USA under the title *Harry Potter and the Sorcerer's Stone*. It was hugely successful. Soon, the book was brought out in many other countries.

In July 1999, the newly-published *Harry Potter and the Prisoner of Azkaban* leapt straight on to the world's bestseller list. Darker than the first two, this volume introduced the Dementors – cruel, black-cloaked prison guards that suck the happiness out of those they capture.

WOW!

By autumn 1999, with three volumes out in the UK and the USA, nearly 30 million Harry Potter titles had been printed.

The poster for the film version of Harry Potter and the Chamber of Secrets *shows Harry, Ron and Hermione.*

Harry on the big screen

By 1999, Jo was constantly busy with interviews, **book signings** and talks. In October, she went on a **book tour** around the USA and was amazed at the enormous crowds that turned out to meet her. She felt like a pop star!

It came as no surprise when Hollywood movie studios expressed an interest in making Harry Potter films. Jo insisted that they be filmed in the UK with real people rather than **animation**.

Jo also wished to approve the **screenplay**. Eventually in 1999, Warner Brothers won the right to make the movie versions. Chris Columbus, the **director** of the first film, promised it would be faithful to the book.

WRITING TIPS

Work hard in your literacy and English lessons at school. You need a good grasp of grammar, punctuation and spelling as a basis to develop your writing skills.

Daniel Radcliffe (left), Emma Watson (centre) and Rupert Grint (right) have starred in all eight films of the seven books.

Girls in Germany show off their copies of Harry Potter and the Goblet of Fire. *German shops started selling the book at the stroke of midnight on 14 October 2000.*

WOW!

The Harry Potter books have sold more than 450 million copies, they have been translated into 70 different languages to date and have been distributed to more than 200 territories around the world.

All of the movies of the books are star-studded, big-budget productions. The young actors who play Harry, Ron and Hermione were between just nine and 11 years old when they were cast in the roles. But the huge success of the films has turned these actors into worldwide celebrities and, in 2009, the film series had made more money than any other in history!

While the first film was getting underway in 2000, Jo continued work on *Harry Potter and the Goblet of Fire*. Bloomsbury decided to publish this title in the UK and the USA on the same date in July 2000. When Jo revealed beforehand that one of the characters would be murdered at the end of the book, 'Pottermania' broke out – a frenzy of excitement to discover Harry's latest adventures.

A quiet celebrity

By 2001 J.K. Rowling was famous worldwide and exceedingly wealthy. She spent some of her time helping charities close to her heart, including the Multiple Sclerosis Society in Scotland and the National Council for One Parent Families (now Gingerbread).

In that year, Jo wrote two short books, *Quidditch Through the Ages* and *Fantastic Beasts and Where to Find Them*. All the profits went to **Comic Relief**. Also in 2001, dramatic changes occurred in Jo's home life. She bought a beautiful mansion in northern Scotland, and she married Neil Murray, a doctor.

Too well known to write in cafés, Jo set up an office at home and started writing *Harry Potter and the Order of the Phoenix*. Her son, David, was born in March 2003, shortly after she finished it. The new title, published

WOW!

J.K.Rowling knew how Harry's story would end years before she came to write the final volume. She wrote the final chapter and locked it in a safe.

In 2000, Jo gave £500,000 to the National Council for One Parent Families (Gingerbread).

in June, was the longest yet. It ran to an incredible 768 pages! Nevertheless, her faithful readers stayed hooked.

Jo gave birth to a second daughter, Mackenzie, in January 2005 but she continued writing. *Harry Potter and the Half-Blood Prince* came out in 2005, and the final volume, *Harry Potter and the Deathly Hallows*, was released in 2007. It sold 15 million copies worldwide in the first 24 hours, breaking sales records as the fastest-selling book ever.

Jo vowed there would be no further Harry Potter titles. In 2008 her collection of fairy tales, *The Tales of Beedle the Bard*, was brought out. Yet she believed that no future books would ever be as successful as Harry Potter.

J.K. Rowling with her husband Neil Murray. Neil works as a doctor.

The impact of J.K. Rowling

J.K Rowling's books have had a huge impact on reading. Her magical world has hooked both children and adults alike, proving that reading can be cool. Many of her readers love Philip Pullman's *Northern Lights* **trilogy** and Stephanie Meyer's vampire romance series *Twilight*.

Once people start reading Harry Potter, it is hard to stop until you reach the end!

Jo's magical world has extended beyond books and film. In 2010, Universal Orlando, in America, opened the Wizarding World of Harry Potter theme park. Visitors can explore Hogwarts Castle, sample Butterbeer and ride a dragon-themed rollercoaster. It is also possible to take a behind-the-scenes tour of the sets, props and costumes used in the films at the Warner Brothers Studio, just outside of London.

New York, 2009: Members of the cast arrive for the premiere of Harry Potter and the Half-Blood Prince.

In 2011, Jo announced plans for her Pottermore website. This interactive site now sells digital editions of the series and offers additional material not previously included in the books. The site has been a huge success for the author, with £3.5 million worth of ebooks sold in its first three months. It seems that whatever J.K. Rowling touches turns to gold, or should that be galleons?

Jo's next project will see her first book for adults published in September 2012. Despite being a world away from the boy with the lightning scar, *The Casual Vacancy* is set to get everyone talking about J.K. Rowlings work once more!

Have you got what it takes to be a writer? Try this

1) How often do you read books?
a) Every day.
b) Often.
c) Rarely.

2) What kind of reading do you do?
a) Anything and everything.
b) I read the books or magazines that I know I'll like.
c) I read what I'm told to read at school.

3) Do you enjoy writing stories?
a) Yes. I have a vivid imagination.
b) Sometimes.
c) No. I only write stories when I'm told to at school.

3) Do you have a good vocabulary and enjoy playing word games?
a) Yes, I love word play.
b) I have a reasonable vocabulary and sometimes play word games.
c) No. I don't really like activities to do with words.

4) How much work do you put into a piece of writing?
a) I plan what to write. Once I've written it, I check it and rewrite the parts I'm not happy with.
b) I read through what I've written once to check for mistakes.
c) I write the piece and that's it!

5) How do you respond when someone criticises your writing?
a) I listen to what they say and try to use it to improve my writing.
b) I listen to what they say but I don't change my work.
c) It makes me upset when people criticise my work.

6) Do you like spending time alone thinking up stories and writing?
a) Yes, I like my own company and using my imagination.
b) Sometimes, but not for too long.
c) No, I get bored – I like to be around other people all the time.

RESULTS

Mostly As: You might have what it takes to be a writer! Keep reading all you can and try to write regularly.

Mostly Bs: You are interested in reading and writing. Search for books that interest and inspire you and try to spend some more time on your writing.

Mostly Cs: Your heart's not really in it! If you'd like to be a writer, start by reading more – not just at school.

Glossary

animation Making a film in which drawings or models of people appear to move.

anti-racist Having beliefs that are against racism and acting to oppose it.

autobiography The story of a person's life, written by that person.

bestseller A book that huge numbers of people buy.

book signing An event at which an author's fans can bring copies of his or her books for the author to sign for them.

book tour A tour by an author, giving talks about his or her work.

civil war A war between groups of people within the same country.

classic A piece of work, such as a book, which is well known and thought to be of a high quality.

Comic Relief A charity that works with entertainers to raise money to help extremely poor people.

compulsion A force that makes somebody do something.

contract An official written agreement.

director A person in charge of making a film who tells the actors and staff what to do.

drafting Making a rough written version of a piece of work that is not yet in its final form.

edit To prepare a piece of writing for publication by correcting the mistakes and improving it.

fantasy Books that use magic as the main theme.

fascist Extreme nationalists who favour a powerful state.

human rights The basic rights that people have to be treated fairly.

literary agent A person who tries to find a publisher who will publish a writer's work.

literature Pieces of writing, such as novels, plays and poems, that are thought to be of high quality.

manuscript The author's copy of a book before it has been printed.

Muggle In the Harry Potter books, someone who is from the non-magical world.

pace In writing, making sure that events don't happen so slowly that the reader grows bored, or so fast that the reader feels they want to know more.

print run The number of books produced in a batch of printing.

reviewer Someone who writes a report in the media giving his or her opinion of a book, play or film.

rights In book publishing, the right to produce a book in another country.

screenplay The words for a film with directions for how it should be acted and filmed.

structure The way in which writing is organised, such as the chapters and scenes.

trilogy A three-book series.

vocabulary The words that a person knows or uses.

welfare benefits Practical help, such as money or services, given to needy people.

Index